Listen, Repeat and Write track 05

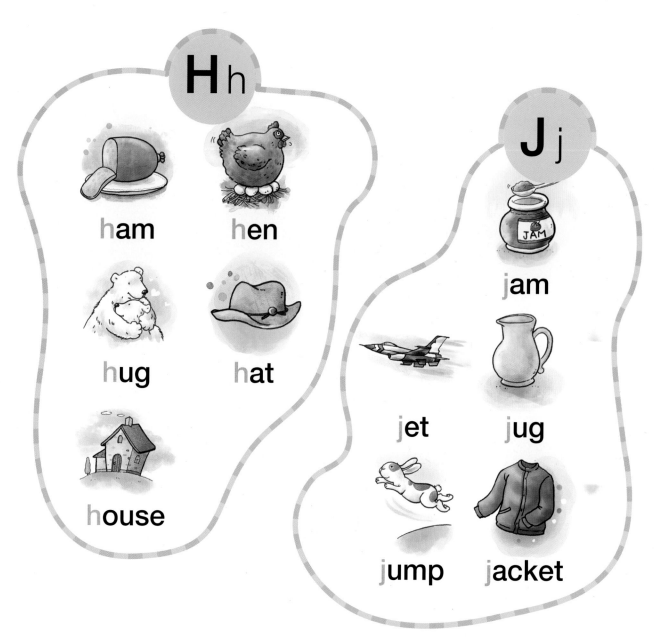

Hh

ham   hen

hug   hat

house

Jj

jam

jet   jug

jump   jacket

 Listen and Circle

1.

2.

Listen and Match

Hh   Jj

 Listen and Make words

1. The man is wearing a and a .

[ ] at   [ ] acket

2. The is flying above the .

[ ] et   [ ] ouse

3. The is in the .

[ ] am   [ ] ug

Listen and Read along

Tom and Jane are playing in the house.

Don't. Don't.

Don't jump in the house.

Sorry. I'm sorry.

I won't jump in the house.

Don't. Don't.

Don't hug the hen.

Sorry. I'm sorry.

I won't hug the hen.

Make a chant

Don't. Don't. Don't _____.

Sorry. I'm sorry. I won't _____.

Find the words that begin with "h" and "j" sound in the chant and circle them.

Unit 5 Consonant Kk·Gg

📖 Judy and Mike are having a party.

Kk

key

kite

kiwi

king

kangaroo

Gg

girl

glass

grape

goat

gorilla

Listen, Repeat and Write track 06

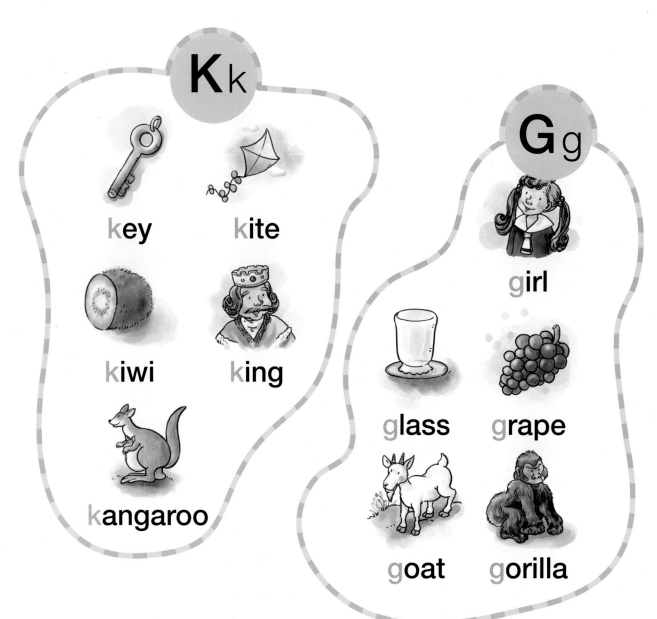

Kk

key   kite

kiwi   king

kangaroo

Gg

girl

glass   grape

goat   gorilla

 Listen and Circle

1.

2.

Listen and Match

 Kk **G**g

 Listen and Make words

1. The likes .

   ☐ irl   ☐ rapes

2. Your is in the .

   ☐ ey   ☐ lass

3. The is flying a .

   ☐ ing   ☐ ite

Listen and Read along

 Tom and Jane are watching the play.

Who has the key?

The king has the key.

The girl has the glass.

Who has the glass?

It was interesting.

Who? Who?

Who has the key?

The king. The king.

The king has the key.

Who? Who?

Who has the glass?

The girl. The girl.

The girl has the glass.

♪ Make a chant

Who? Who? Who has the _____?

The _____. The _____.

The _____ has the _____.

♪ Find the words that begin with "k" and "g" sound in the chant and circle them.

Unit 6 Consonant Mm · Nn

📖 Mike is cleaning the house with his sister, Mary.

Mm

map   man   mat   mop   mud

Nn

net   nun   nuts   nest   nail

Listen, Repeat and Write track 07

Mm

map   man

mat   mop

mud

Nn

net

nun   nuts

nest   nail

 Listen and Circle

1.

2.

 Listen and Match

Mm   Nn

 Listen and Make words

1. The is looking at the .

☐ un   ☐ ap

2. There is on the .

☐ ud   ☐ et

3. The likes .

☐ an   ☐ uts

Listen and Read along

 Tom and Jane went to the store to buy something.

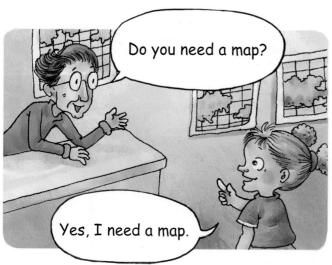

Do you need a map?

Yes, I need a map.

Do you need a nail?

No, I don't need a nail.

Do you need?

Do you need a map?

Yes. Yes, I need a map.

Do you need?

Do you need a nail?

No. No, I don't need a nail.

Make a chant

Do you need? Do you need a _____?

Yes. Yes, I need a _____.

(No. No, I don't need a _____.)

Find the words that begin with "m" and "n" sound in the chant and circle them.

Review

1 Listen and circle the first letter. track 08

Hh   Jj

Hh   Jj

Gg   Kk

Gg   Kk

Mm   Nn

Mm   Nn

2 Listen and write the letter.

____ ump

____ ug

____ op

3 Circle the beginning sound.

k g h   m n h   k g j

m n h   m n h   k g j

4 Circle the correct picture.

Nn

Kk

Gg

5 Listen and fill in the blanks.

1. Don't. Don't. Don't _____ump in the _____ouse.

   Sorry. I'm sorry. I won't _____ump in the _____ouse.

   Don't. Don't. Don't _____ug the _____en.

   Sorry. I'm sorry. I won't _____ug the _____en.

2. Who? Who? Who has the _____ey?

   The _____ing. The _____ing. The _____ing has the _____ey.

   Who? Who? Who has the _____lass?

   The _____irl. The _____irl. The _____irl has the _____lass.

3. Do you need? Do you need a _____ap?

   Yes. Yes, I need a _____ap.

   Do you need? Do you need a _____ail?

   No. No, I don't need a _____ail.

Let's Play A Game

Play tic-tac-toe game with your partner.

_____at	_____am	_____op	_____en
_____un	_____et	_____et	_____ap
_____ey	_____ing	_____irl	_____ail
_____ud	_____lass	_____ite	_____ug

How to Play:

1. Choose a square.

2. Say the name of the picture that you chose. Then, complete the word.

3. When you complete the word, put a check mark on the picture. If you can't, do not put a check mark.

4. Take turns choosing squares and continue the game.

5. The one who gets four in a row wins.

 **Unit 7** Consonant **Ll · Rr**

📖 James and Judy are in the living room.

Ll

 lock   lion    lily   lamp   lemon

Rr

 red   ring    rug   robot   rabbit

Listen, Repeat and Write track 09

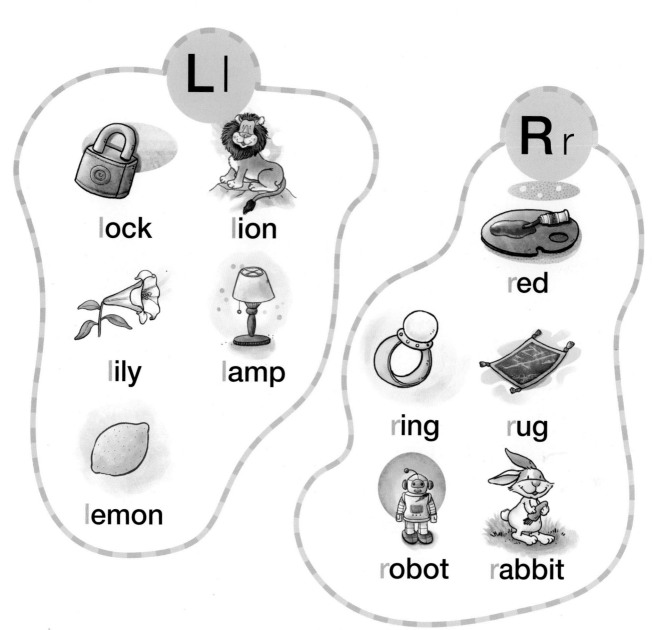

Ll

lock   lion

lily   lamp

lemon

Rr

red

ring   rug

robot   rabbit

 Listen and Circle

1.

2.

Listen and Match

Ll

Rr

 Listen and Make words

1. Jim gives Helen a and a .

[ ] ily   [ ] ing

2. The is standing on the .

[ ] amp   [ ] ug

3. He is drawing a   .

[ ] ed   [ ] abbit

Listen and Read along

 Tom and Jane are helping each other.

> Is the ring on the rug?

> Yes. The ring is on the rug.

> Is the lock on the lamp?

> No. The lock isn't on the lamp.

The ring? The ring?

Is the ring on the rug?

Yes. Yes.

The ring is on the rug.

The lock? The lock?

Is the lock on the lamp?

No. No.

The lock isn't on the lamp.

> Thank you.

♪ Make a chant

The _____. The _____.

Is the _____ on the _____?

Yes. Yes. The _____ is on the _____.

(No. No. The _____ isn't

on the _____.)

♪ Find the words that begin with "l" and "r" sound in the chant and circle them.

Unit 8 Consonant Ss · Zz

📖 Judy went to the beach with her family.

Ss

sun　　　sea　　　sky　　　sand　　　sleep

Zz

zoo　　　zero　　　zigzag　　　zipper　　　zebra

Listen, Repeat and Write track 10

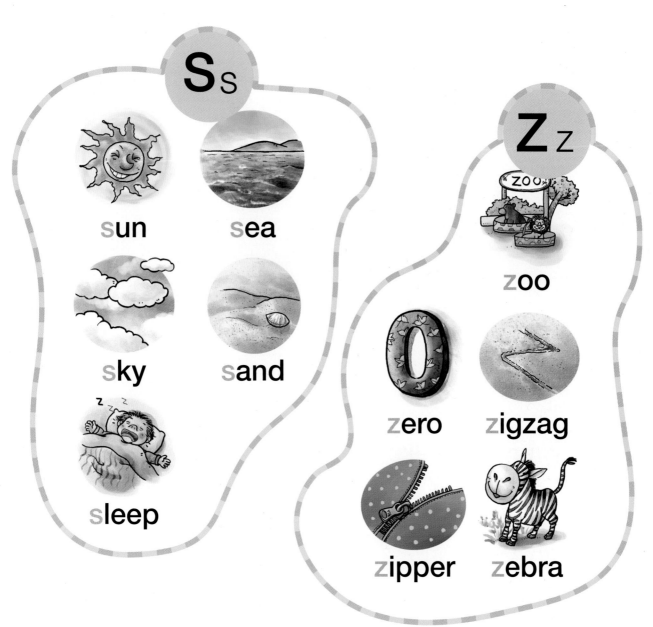

Ss

sun   sea

sky   sand

sleep

Zz

zoo

zero   zigzag

zipper   zebra

 Listen and Circle

1.

2.

 Listen and Match

 S s   Z z

 Listen and Make words

1. The is shining in the .

           un   ky

2. The is running on the .

           ebra   and

3. Run in and write the number .

           igzag   ero

Listen and Read along

 Tom and Jane answer their teacher's question.

The sun. The sun.

Where can you see the sun?

In the sky. In the sky.

I can see the sun in the sky.

The zebra. The zebra.

Where can you see the zebra?

In the zoo. In the zoo.

I can see the zebra in the zoo.

♪ Make a chant

The _____. The _____.
Where can you see the _____?
In the _____. In the _____.
I can see the _____ in the _____.

♪ Find the words that begin with "s" and "z" sound in the chant and circle them.

Consonant Cc · Qq

 Mike is eating out with his mom.

Cc

 cup

 cat

 cap

 car

Qq

 queen

 circle

 circus

 cinema

 cereal

 quilt

Listen, Repeat and Write track 11

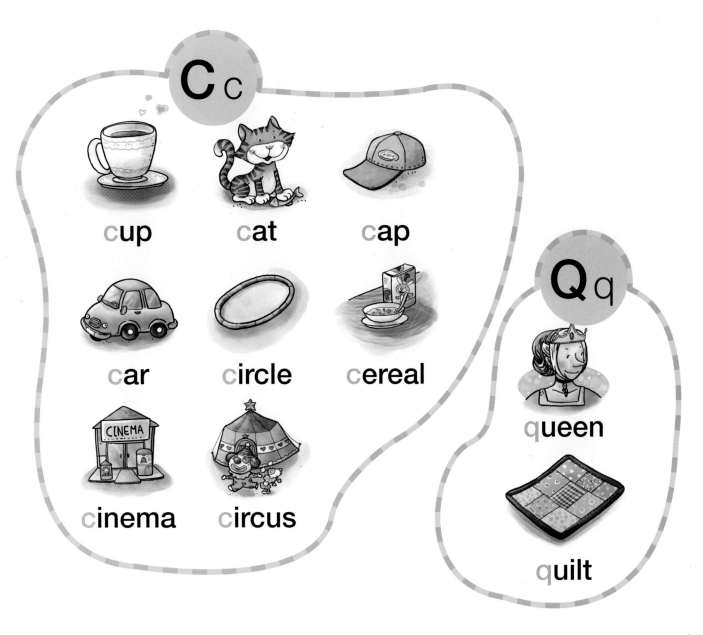

C c

cup

cat

cap

car

circle

cereal

cinema

circus

Q q

queen

quilt

 Listen and Circle

1.

2.

Listen and Match

 Cc

Qq

 Listen and Make words

1. The is running to the .

☐ at   ☐ ar

2. Will you go to the or ?

☐ ircus ☐ inema

3. The gives the boy a .

☐ ueen   ☐ uilt

Listen and Read along

 Mom is angry because Tom and Jane quarreled.

This is my cap.
You can't wear my cap.

This is my quilt.
You can't use my quilt.

My cap. My cap.

This is my cap.

You can't. You can't.

You can't wear my cap.

My quilt. My quilt.

This is my quilt.

You can't. You can't.

You can't use my quilt.

This is my cereal.
You can't eat my cereal.

Make a chant

My _____. My _____.
This is my _____.
You can't. You can't.
You can't wear/use my _____.

Find the words that begin with "c" and "q" sound in the chant and circle them.

1 Listen and circle the first letter. track 12

Ss Zz

Ll Rr

Cc Qq

Ll Rr

Ss Zz

Cc Qq

2 Listen and write the letter.

___ ky

___ ily

___ ircle

3 Circle the beginning sound.

c   s   z

c   s   q

l   r   z

c   s   q

l   r   z

c   s   z

4 Circle the correct picture.

Cc

Rr

Zz

5 Listen and fill in the blanks.

1. The _____ing? The _____ing? Is the _____ing on the _____ug?

   Yes. Yes. The _____ing is on the _____ug.

   The _____ock? The _____ock? Is the _____ock on the _____amp?

   No. No. The _____ock isn't on the _____amp.

2. The _____un. The _____un. Where can you see the _____un?

   In the _____ky. In the _____ky. I can see the _____un in the

   _____ky.

   The _____ebra. The _____ebra. Where can you see the _____ebra?

   In the _____oo. In the _____oo. I can see the _____ebra in the

   _____oo.

3. My _____ap. My _____ap. This is my _____ap.

   You can't. You can't. You can't wear my _____ap.

   My _____uilt. My _____uilt. This is my _____uilt.

   You can't. You can't. You can't use my _____uilt.

Let's Play A Game

Play a board game with your partner. You need picture cards(C set).

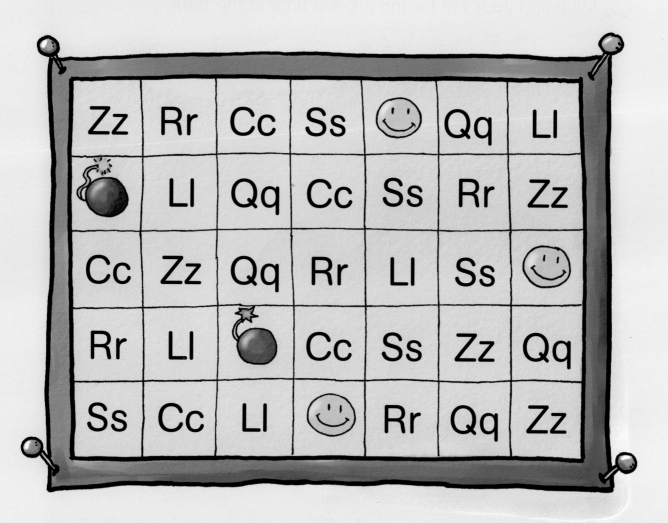

Zz	Rr	Cc	Ss	☺	Qq	Ll
💣	Ll	Qq	Cc	Ss	Rr	Zz
Cc	Zz	Qq	Rr	Ll	Ss	☺
Rr	Ll	💣	Cc	Ss	Zz	Qq
Ss	Cc	Ll	☺	Rr	Qq	Zz

 How to Play:

1. Spread the picture cards around the board and place a coin in a corner.

2. Flick the coin and sound out the letter where the coin lands on.

3. Take a matching picture card and speak out what is on the picture.

4. The winner is the one who gets the most cards.

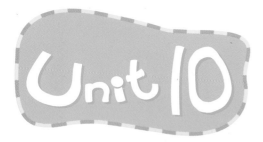 **Consonant** W w • Y y • X x

Mike and Judy are having a good time in the park.

W w   Y y   X x

wig   web   yo-yo   yellow   fox

wind   watch   yacht   box   six

Listen, Repeat and Write track 13

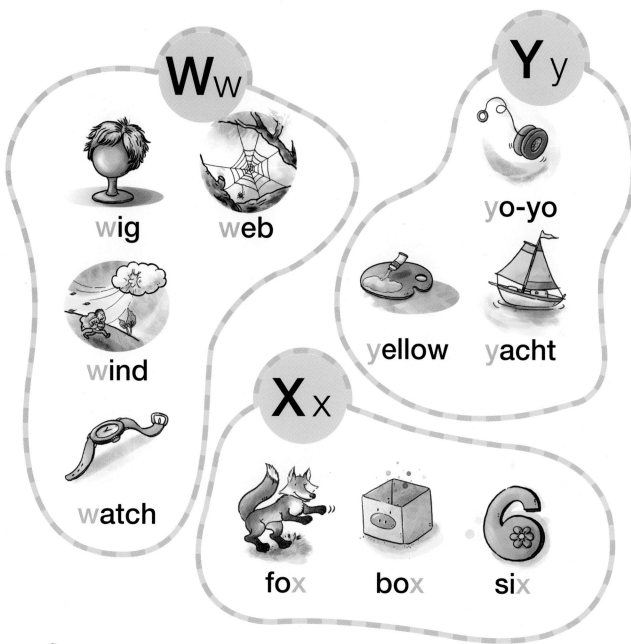

Ww

wig   web

wind

watch

Yy

yo-yo

yellow   yacht

Xx

fox   box   six

 Listen and Circle

1.

2.

Listen and Match

Ww   Yy

 Listen and Make words

1. My  is .

     o-yo   ellow

2. The  is behind the  .

   fo   bo

3. The woman has   .

   si   igs

Listen and Read along

 Tom and Jane made a mess in their house.

> Whose watch is this?
>
> The watch is Jane's.

> Whose yo-yo is this?
>
> The yo-yo is Tom's.

> Whose box is this?
>
> The box is ours.

A watch. A watch.

Whose watch is this?

Jane's. Jane's.

The watch is Jane's.

A yo-yo. A yo-yo.

Whose yo-yo is this?

Tom's. Tom's.

The yo-yo is Tom's.

♪ **Make a chant**

A _____. A _____.
Whose _____ is this?
_____'s. _____'s.
The _____ is _____'s.

♪ Find the words that begin with "w" and "y" sound in the chant and circle them.

Unit 11 Short Vowel Aa

📖 Judy went on a picnic with her family.

Aa

ant

apple

ax

arrow

actor

rat

bat

can

van

dam

Listen, Repeat and Write track 14

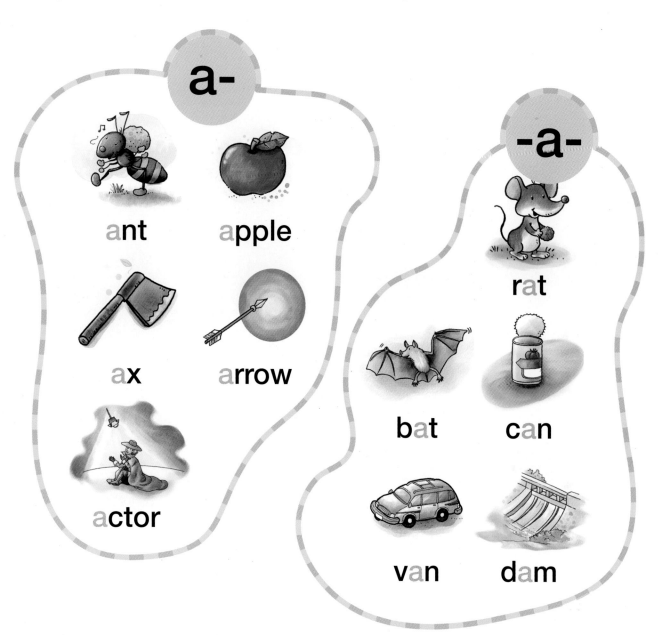

a-

ant   apple

ax   arrow

actor

-a-

rat

bat   can

van   dam

 Listen and Circle

1.

2.

Listen, Write and Match

_____nt   c_____n   _____pple   _____ctor

 Listen and Make words

1. Which do you need? An or an ?

    [ ] x   [ ] rrow

2. The  is near the .

    v [ ] n   d [ ] m

3. I hate and  .

    r [ ] ts   b [ ] ts

Tom and Jane are afraid of ants and bats.

Ants. Ants.

They are ants.

I don't like ants.

I hate ants.

Bats. Bats.

They are bats.

I don't like bats.

I hate bats.

♪ Make a chant

_____(e)s. _____(e)s.

They are _____(e)s.

I don't like _____(e)s.

I hate _____(e)s.

♪ Find the words that have short "a" sound in the chant and circle them.

Unit 12 Short Vowel Ee

📖 Judy and Mike went to the zoo with their friends.

elephant   egg   elevator   elbow   empty

Ee

leg   ten   wet   pet   yell

Listen, Repeat and Write track 15

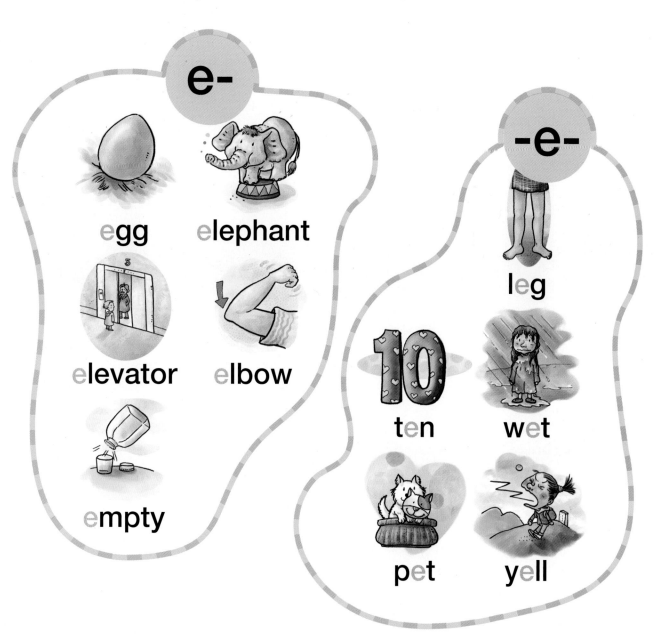

e-

egg   elephant

elevator   elbow

empty

-e-

leg

ten   wet

pet   yell

 Listen and Circle

1.

2.

Listen, Write and Match

w_____t   p_____t   y_____ll   _____mpty

 Listen and Make words

1. I have  .

   t [ ] n   [ ] ggs

2. The is in the .

   [ ] lephant   [ ] levator

3. My and hurt.

   l [ ] gs   [ ] lbows

Listen and Read along

 Tom and Jane got hurt.

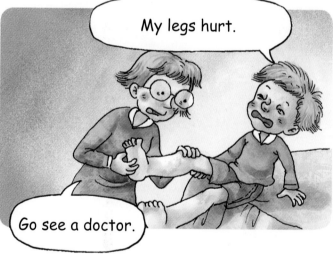

Elbows. My elbows.

My elbows hurt.

Go. Go.

Go see a doctor.

Legs. My legs.

My legs hurt.

Go. Go.

Go see a doctor.

♪ Make a chant

_____(e)s. My _____(e)s.

My _____(e)s hurt.

Go. Go. Go see a doctor.

♪ Find the words that have short "e" sound in the chant and circle them.

1 Listen and write the letter. 🎧 track 16

☐ ig

si ☐

☐ acht

l ☐ g

☐ x

d ☐ m

2 Listen and circle the first letter. 🎧

Ww **X**x

Ww **Y**y

Aa **E**e

Circle the correct word.

box
boy
boz

ven
van
vin

ten
tan
tin

rit
ret
rat

wat
wet
wot

pet
pit
pot

 Circle the correct picture.

Ww

Aa

Ee

5 Listen and fill in the blanks.

1. A _____atch. A _____atch. Whose _____atch is this?

Jane's. Jane's. The _____atch is Jane's.

A _____o-yo. A _____o-yo. Whose _____o-yo is this?

Tom's. Tom's. The _____o-yo is Tom's.

2. _____nts. _____nts. They are _____nts.

I don't like _____nts. I hate _____nts.

B_____ts. B_____ts. They are b_____ts.

I don't like b_____ts. I hate b_____ts.

3. _____lbows. My _____lbows. My _____lbows hurt.

Go. Go. Go see a doctor.

L_____gs. My l_____gs. My l_____gs hurt.

Go. Go. Go see a doctor.

Let's Play A Game

Play a game with your partner.

 How to Play:

1. Make word cards using the words that you learned in Unit 10, Unit 11, Unit 12.

2. Spread the word cards that you made on the desk.

3. A teacher chooses a flash card randomly. Then the teacher reads the card out loud.

4. Listen to the word your teacher says. Then try to be the first student to touch the correct word card. The first student takes the word card.

5. The student who gets the most cards wins.

Unit 13 Short Vowel Ii

 There was a bazaar in the village.

I i

ink

iguana

igloo

indian

insect

sit

hit

dig

mix

sing

Listen, Repeat and Write track 17

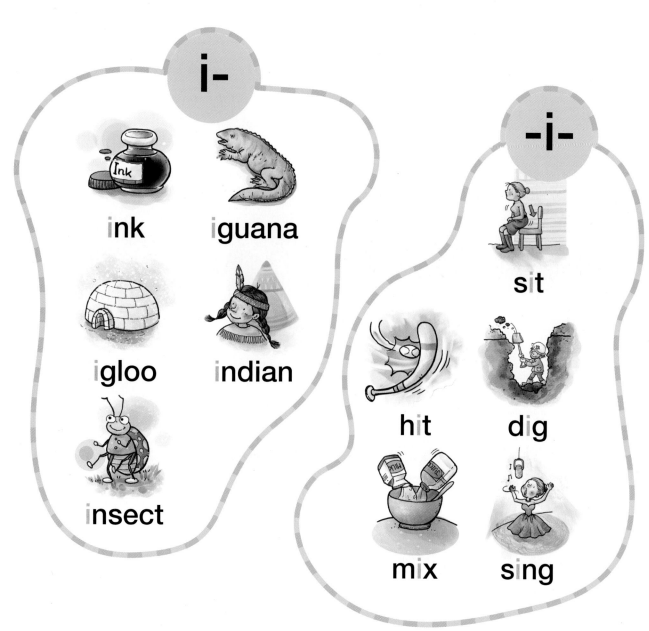

i-

ink   iguana

igloo   indian

insect

-i-

sit

hit   dig

mix   sing

 Listen and Circle

1.

2.

Listen, Write and Match

d____g   m____x   h____t   ____guana

 Listen and Make words

1. Don't on the .

s___t   ___gloo

2. The likes to .

___ndian s___ng

3. He is drawing an in .

___nsect   ___nk

Listen and Read along

 Tom and Jane are enjoying their hobbies.

> I can hit a ball.
> It's fun to hit a ball.

> I can sing a song.
> It's fun to sing a song.

> Troublemakers!

Hit. Hit.

I can hit a ball.

Fun. Fun.

It's fun to hit a ball.

Sing. Sing.

I can sing a song.

Fun. Fun.

It's fun to sing a song.

♪ Make a chant

_____. _____.

I can _____.

Fun. Fun. It's fun to _____.

♪ Find the words that have short "i" sound in the chant and circle them.

 Judy visits her grandfather.

O o

 ox

 owl

 octopus

 ostrich

 october

 mom

 hot

 rock

 sock

 clock

Listen, Repeat and Write track 18

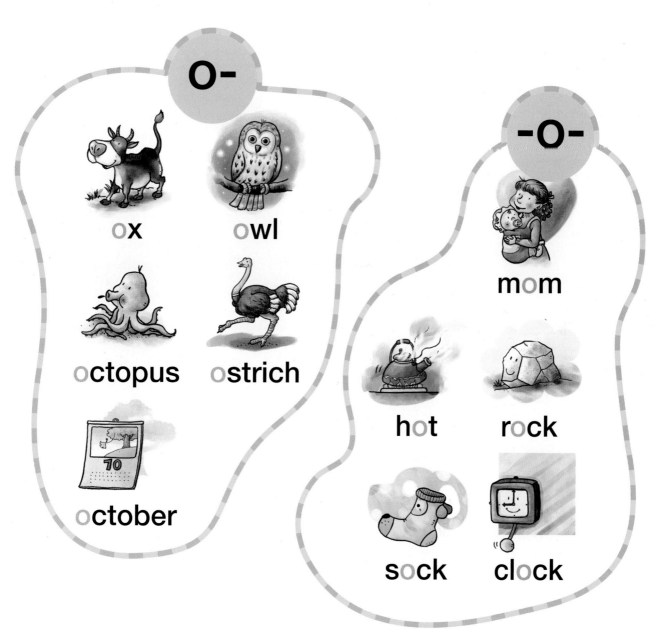

O-

ox

owl

octopus

ostrich

october

-O-

mom

hot

rock

sock

clock

 Listen and Circle

1.

2.

Listen, Write and Match

s_____ck   cl_____ck   _____ctober   _____ctopus

 Listen and Make words

1.   is drinking a cup of coffee.

M ☐ m   h ☐ t

2. The is kicking a .

☐ x   r ☐ ck

3.  can fly, but can not fly.

☐ wls   ☐ striches

Listen and Read along

 Tom and Jane are looking at the birds in the zoo.

> An owl is a bird.
> It can fly.

Owl. Owl.

It is an owl.

An owl is a bird.

It can fly.

Ostrich. Ostrich.

It is an ostrich.

An ostrich is a bird.

It can not fly.

> An ostrich is a bird.
> It can not fly.

Make a chant

_____. _____.

It is a/an _____.

A/An _____ is a bird.

It can fly. (It can not fly.)

> I am faster than a bird.

Find the words that have short "o" sound in the chant and circle them.

Unit 15 Short Vowel Uu

 Mike went shopping with his uncle.

umbrella   uncle   underwear   ugly   unhappy

Uu

  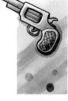 

gum   mug   cut   gun   run

Listen, Repeat and Write track 19

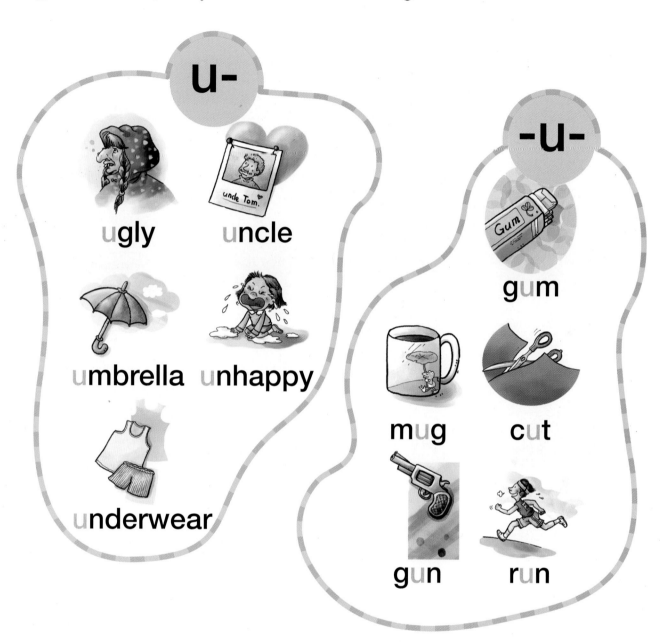

u-

ugly   uncle

umbrella   unhappy

underwear

-u-

gum

mug   cut

gun   run

 Listen and Circle

1.

2.

Listen, Write and Match

c____t   g____m   m____g   ____nderwear

·   ·   ·   ·

·   ·   ·   ·

 Listen and Make words

1. The woman is .

☐ gly   ☐ nhappy

2. My is holding an  .

☐ ncle   ☐ mbrella

3. Don't  with a .

r ☐ n   g ☐ n

Listen and Read along

 Tom and Jane buy new things.

How much is the umbrella?

The umbrella is $10.

How much? How much?

How much is the umbrella?

Umbrella. Umbrella.

The umbrella is $10.

How much? How much?

How much is the mug?

Mug. Mug.

The mug is $5.

How much is the mug?

The mug is $5.

♪ Make a chant

How much? How much?

How much is the _____?

_____. _____.

The _____ is $_____.

♪ Find the words that have short "u" sound in the chant and circle them.

1 Listen and write the letter. track 20

 nk

 wl

 ncle

 s t

 m m

 g m

2 Listen and circle the first letter.

Ii   Oo

Oo   Uu

Oo   Uu

3 Circle the correct word.

dig
dog
dug

hit
hot
hut

rin
ron
run

cit
cot
cut

hit
hot
hut

sick
sock
suck

4 Circle the correct picture.

I i

O o

U u

5 Listen and fill in the blanks.

1. H_____t. H_____t. I can h_____t a ball.

   Fun. Fun. It's fun to h_____t a ball.

   S_____ng. S_____ng. I can s_____ng a song.

   Fun. Fun. It's fun to s_____ng a song.

2. _____wl. _____wl. It is an _____wl.

   An _____wl is a bird. It can fly.

   _____strich. _____strich. It is an _____strich.

   An _____strich is a bird. It can not fly.

3. How much? How much? How much is the _____mbrella?

   _____mbrella. _____mbrella. The _____mbrella is $10.

   How much? How much? How much is the m_____g?

   M_____g. M_____g. The m_____g is $5.

Let's Play A Game

Play a game with your partner.

 How to Play:

1. Make a dice from the appendix.

2. Take turns throwing the dice.

3. Make a word which has the sound shown on the dice. For example, if your dice shows "i", make a word that has "i" sound like "ink."

4. If you make a correct word, you get 5 points. If you can't, you lose 3 points.

5. The winner is the one who gets the most points.

게임 방법

Review (page 21)

준비물: 주사위, 그림 카드(A세트)

1. 주사위를 준비한다. 카드를 뒤집어 쌓아 놓는다.
2. 번갈아 가며 주사위를 던진다.
3. 주사위를 던진 다음 카드를 뽑아 영어로 똑바로 발음한다.
4. 제대로 발음을 하면 자신이 던진 주사위 숫자만큼 점수를 얻는다. 제대로 발음을 못하면 점수를 못 얻는다.
5. 점수를 제일 많이 얻은 사람이 승자이다.

Review (page 37)

준비물: 연필, 빙고판

1. 빙고판에 있는 그림 하나를 선택한 다음, 그림이 나타내는 단어를 영어로 말한다.
2. 그림을 영어로 말한 다음, 빈칸에 맞는 알파벳을 연필로 써서 단어를 완성한다.
3. 단어를 맞게 완성하면 그림에 체크를 한다. 그렇지 못하면 그림에 체크할 수 없다.
4. 번갈아 가며 그림을 선택하면서 게임을 계속 이어 간다.
5. 가로, 세로, 혹은 대각선으로 4열을 체크하면 이긴다.

Review (page 53)

준비물: 그림 카드(C세트), 동전

1. 게임판을 책상 위에 놓고 그림 카드를 게임판 주위에 잘 보이게 펼쳐 놓는다. 동전을 게임판 모퉁이 아무 데나 놓는다.
2. 동전을 튕겨 동전이 떨어진 곳의 글자를 보고 그 글자로 시작되는 단어 카드를 고른다.
3. 해당되는 그림 카드를 한 장 가져가며 소리와 단어를 말한다. (즉, 고양이 그림을 가져갈 경우 c-cat이라고 말한다.)
4. 그림 카드를 많이 모으는 사람이 승자가 된다. 참고로, 웃는 얼굴에 동전이 떨어지면 아무 카드나 가지고 갈 수 있고, 폭탄에 떨어지면 한 번을 쉬어야 한다.

Review (page 69)

준비물: 단어 카드

1. 먼저 학생들에게 11과, 12과, 13과에 나오는 단어를 종이에 써서 단어 카드를 만들게 한다.
2. 학생들이 만든 카드를 책상에 펼쳐 놓게 한다.
3. 선생님이 그림 카드를 보여 주며 단어를 말한다.
4. 선생님이 말하는 그림에 해당하는 단어 카드를 먼저 고르는 사람이 가져간다.
5. 카드를 제일 많이 가져간 사람이 승자이다.

Review (page 85)

준비물: 주사위

1. 부록으로 실린 주사위를 오려 만든다.
2. 돌아가면서 주사위를 던진다.
3. 던진 면이 나타내는 알파벳이 들어간 단어를 말한다.
4. 단어를 말하면 점수를 5점씩 얻는다. 올바른 단어를 만들지 못하면 3점씩 깎인다.
5. 점수를 제일 많이 얻은 사람이 승자이다.

Ll	Zz	🙂	Qq	Zz
Qq	Rr	Ss	Zz	Qq
🙂	Ss	Ll	Ss	Rr
Ss	Cc	Rr	Cc	🙂
Cc	Qq	Qq	💣	Ll
Rr	Ll	Zz	Ll	Cc
Zz	💣	Cc	Rr	Ss

Picture Cards   A set

Picture Cards

B set

Picture Cards

C set

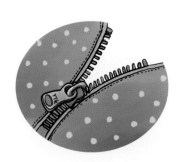

Picture Cards

C set

Picture Cards

D set

Picture Cards

E set

uncle Tom.

Gum

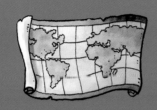

Put wings on your phonics!

Wing Wing

2

Phonics

Workbook

Single Letter Sounds

Nexus Contents Development Team

NEXUS Edu

Put wings on your phonics!

Phonics

Wing Wing

2

Single Letter Sounds

Nexus Contents Development Team

Workbook

NEXUS Edu

 Match each word with the correct picture.
Then write the word.

p + ot   ·   ·      _____

b + ag   ·   ·      _____

b + at   ·   ·      _____

p + ie   ·   ·      _____

Write the first letter of the word.

_____

_____

_____

_____

_____

_____

Look at the picture and match the words.

pan pot pie pig plum

bus bat bed box bag

 Choose the correct word and write.

1. Look at the _____ over there.

bus, pan

2. There is a _____ on the _____.

bat, pie   pig, bed

3. Watch out! The _____ is hot.

bag, pot

4

Choose the right picture.

bag

pot

plum

 Choose the word beginning with a different letter.

1.

2.

Match each word with the correct picture.
Then write the word.

t + ub ·

·  _____

d + og ·

·  _____

t + ent ·

·  _____

d + ad ·

·  _____

Write the first letter of the word.

_____

_____

_____

_____

_____

_____

Look at the picture and match the words.

tree tent tub taxi truck

dad doll dish dog duck

 Choose the correct word and write.

1. Where can I take a  _____?

taxi, truck

2. The _____ is on the table.

duck, dish

3. My _____ is sleeping under the _____.

dog, tub   doll, tree

8

Choose the right picture.

duck

truck

dish

 Choose the word beginning with a different letter.

1.

2.

✏️ Match each word with the correct picture.
Then write the word.

v + **an** ·   ·  _____

f + **an** ·   ·  _____

f + **ox** ·   ·  _____

v + **ase** ·   ·  _____

Write the first letter of the word.

_____
_____
_____

_____
_____
_____

Look at the picture and match the words.

fan fox fly frog fish

van vest vine vase violin

 Choose the correct word and write.

1. Where can I find a _____?

fan, van

2. There is a _____ in the _____.

fox, frog   violin, vine

3. He is wearing a _____.

vest, fish

12

Choose the right picture.

fish

vase

vine

 Choose the word beginning with a different letter.

1.

2.

 Match each word with the correct picture.
Then write the word.

j + et ·

·  _____

h + at ·

·  _____

j + am ·

·  _____

h + en ·

·  _____

Write the first letter of the word.

_____
_____
_____

_____
_____
_____

_____
_____
_____

_____
_____
_____

_____
_____
_____

_____
_____
_____

Look at the picture and match the words.

ham hen hug hat house

jam jet jug jump jacket

 Choose the correct word and write.

1. I want to eat a _____ sandwich.

ham, jam

2. Don't _____ in the classroom.

hug, jump

3. I don't like the _____. I will take the _____.

hat, jet   house, jacket

16

Choose the right picture.

jug

hug

hat

 Choose the word beginning with a different letter.

1.

2.

Unit 5   Consonant Kk · Gg

 Match each word with the correct picture.
Then write the word.

k + ey ·   ·    _____

g + irl ·   ·    _____

k + ite ·   ·    _____

g + oat ·   ·    _____

Write the first letter of the word.

_____

_____

_____

_____

_____

_____

Look at the picture and match the words.

key kite kiwi king kangaroo

 Choose the correct word and write.

1. There is a _____ on the dish.

kite, kiwi

2. I can't find my _____.

key, girl

3. The _____ wants to eat _____ s.

gorilla, kangaroo   glass, grape

Choose the right picture.

kite			
girl			
goat			

 Choose the word beginning with a different letter.

1.

2.

✏️ Match each word with the correct picture.
Then write the word.

m + an ·   ·  _____

n + et ·   ·  _____

m + at ·   ·  _____

n + un ·   ·  _____

Write the first letter of the word.

_____
_____
_____

_____
_____
_____

Look at the picture and match the words.

map man mat mop mud

net nun nuts nest nail

 Choose the correct word and write.

1. Look at the _____.

nest, mud

2. It's dirty. Do you have a _____?

net, mop

3. The _____ is eating _____.

nun, man   map, nuts

Choose the right picture.

map

net

mud

 Choose the word beginning with a different letter.

1.

2.

Match each word with the correct picture.
Then write the word.

r + ed ·　　·　　_____

l + amp ·　　·　　_____

l + ock ·　　·　　_____

r + ing ·　　·　　_____

Write the first letter of the word.

_____

_____

_____

_____

_____

_____

Look at the picture and match the words.

lock lion lily lamp lemon

red ring rug robot rabbit

 Choose the correct word and write.

1. The _____ is sleeping on the _____.

    rabbit, lion   rug, lamp

2. The _____ _____ is so beautiful!

    red, lock   ring, lily

3. I need to buy a _____ and a _____.

    lamp, robot   rabbit, lemon

28

Choose the right picture.

lion

lemon

ring

 Choose the word beginning with a different letter.

1.

2.

 Match each word with the correct picture.
Then write the word.

s + **ky** ·

·  _____

z + **oo** ·

·  _____

s + **ea** ·

·  _____

z + **ero** ·

·  _____

Write the first letter of the word.

_____
_____
_____

_____
_____
_____

Look at the picture and match the words.

sun sea sky sand sleep

zoo zero zebra zigzag zipper

 Choose the correct word and write.

1. Look at the _____ in the _____!

           sun, zero   sea, sky

2. There is a _____ in the _____.

        zebra, zigzag   sand, zoo

3. The boy is writing a _____ in the _____.

         zero, sleep   sand, zipper

Choose the right picture.

sea

sand

zipper

 Choose the word beginning with a different letter.

1.

2.

Unit 9

Consonant Cc • Qq

 Match each word with the correct picture.
Then write the word.

c + up ·

· _____

c + at ·

· _____

c + ar ·

· _____

c + ap ·

· _____

Write the first letter of the word.

_____
_____
_____

_____
_____
_____

_____
_____
_____

_____
_____
_____

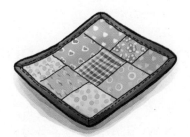

_____
_____
_____

_____
_____
_____

Look at the picture and match the words.

cup cat cap car circle

circus cinema cereal queen quilt

 Choose the correct word and write them.

1. The _____ is wearing a _____.

car, cat   cap, cup

2. The _____ is making a _____.

queen, circle   cereal, quilt

3. I will go to the _____ by _____.

circus, cinema   cup, car

Choose the right picture.

cap

queen

circus

 Choose the word beginning with a different letter.

1.

  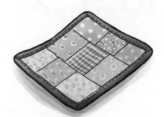

2.

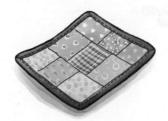  

Match each word with the correct picture.
Then write the word.

w + ig ·  · _____

bo + x ·  · _____

fo + x ·  · _____

si + x ·  · _____

Write the first letter of the word.

_____
_____
_____

_____
_____
_____

_____
_____
_____

_____
_____
_____

_____
_____
_____

_____
_____
_____

Look at the picture and match the words.

wig web wind watch box

fox six yo-yo yellow yacht

 Choose the correct word and write.

1. Your _____ is in the _____.

wind, watch   fox, box

2. I have _____ _____s.

wig, six   yo-yo, yellow

3. There is a _____ above the _____.

six, web   fox, yacht

40

Choose the right picture.

wig

six

yacht

 Choose the word beginning with a different letter.

1.

2.

Unit 11 Short Vowel Aa

 Match each word with the correct picture.
Then write the word.

a + nt ·   ·  _____

r + at ·   ·  _____

b + at ·   ·  _____

d + am ·   ·  _____

Choose the correct word.

apple ı **epple**

ox ı **ax**

van ı **vin**

urrow ı **arrow**

actor ı **ictor**

can ı **cun**

Look at the picture and match the words.

ant apple ax arrow actor

rat bat can van dam

 Choose the correct word and write.

1. There is an _____ under the _____ tree.

ax, rat   apple, actor

2. Can you see the _____ on the _____?

can, dam   bat, van

3. An _____ is crossing the _____.

bat, ant   dam, van

Choose the right picture.

ax

rat

apple

 Choose the word without short "a" vowel.

1.

2.

Unit 12 Short Vowel Ee

 Match each word with the correct picture.
Then write the word.

e + gg ·   ·  _____

l + eg ·   ·  _____

w + et ·   ·  _____

t + en ·   ·  _____

Choose the correct word.

umpty ı **e**mpty

elephant ı **o**lephant

alevator ı **e**levator

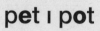

p**e**t ı p**o**t

yill ı **y**ell

elbow ı **u**lbow

Look at the picture and match the words.

egg elephant elevator elbow empty

leg ten wet pet yell

 Choose the correct word and write.

1. The _____ is _____ .

   elephant, elevator   ten, wet

2. The _____ is _____ .

   elephant, elevator   elbow, empty

3. My _____s are playing with an _____ .

   pet, leg   yell, egg

48

Choose the right picture.

leg

empty

yell

 Choose the word without short "e" vowel.

1.

2.

Match each word with the correct picture.
Then write the word.

i + nk ·

·  _____

s + it ·

·  _____

d + ig ·

·  _____

m + ix ·

·  _____

Choose the correct word.

agloo ı **i**gloo

indian ı **u**ndian

s**e**ng ı s**i**ng

oguana ı **i**guana

insect ı **e**nsect

h**u**t ı h**i**t

Look at the picture and match the words.

ink iguana igloo indian insect

sit hit dig mix sing

 Choose the correct word and write.

1. Don't _____ near my _____.

   mix, sing   igloo, indian

2. An _____ is _____ting in the tree.

   igloo, iguana   hit, sit

3. An _____ is _____ging a hole.

   insect, indian   mix, dig

Choose the right picture.

indian

insect

sit

 Choose the word without short "i" vowel.

1.

2.

Unit 14 Short Vowel Oo

  Match each word with the correct picture.
Then write the word.

o + wl ·

·  _____

m + om ·

·  _____

h + ot ·

·  _____

r + ock ·

·  _____

Choose the correct word.

ox I **a**x

uctopus I **o**ctopus

s**a**ck I s**o**ck

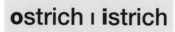

ostrich I **i**strich

uctober I **o**ctober

cl**o**ck I cl**u**ck

Look at the picture and match the words.

ox owl octopus ostrich october

mom hot rock sock clock

 Choose the correct word and write.

1. My _____ s are on the _____ .

   sock, hot   clock, rock

2. The _____ is eating an _____ .

   ox, owl   ostrich, octopus

3. My _____ is buying a _____ .

   owl, mom   clock, rock

56

Choose the right picture.

owl

ostrich

clock

 Choose the word without short "o" vowel.

1.

2.

Short Vowel Uu

 Match each word with the correct picture.
Then write the word.

g + um ·

· _____

m + ug ·

· _____

r + un ·

· _____

c + ut ·

Gum

· _____

Choose the correct word.

oncle ı **u**ncle

umbrella ı **a**mbrella

enderwear ı **u**nderwear

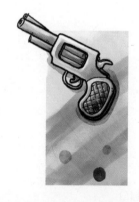

gun ı **gin**

inhappy ı **u**nhappy

egly ı **u**gly

Look at the picture and match the words.

ugly uncle umbrella underwear unhappy

gum mug cut gun run

 Choose the correct word and write.

1. My _____ is chewing _____.

   uncle, ugly   gum, gun

2. The _____ woman buys an _____.

   uncle, ugly   underwear, umbrella

3. The _____ girl _____ her hair.

   ugly, unhappy   cut, run

60

Choose the right picture.

uncle

umbrella

run

 Choose the word without short "u"vowel.

1.

2.

memo~

memo~

Wing Wing Phonics 2

Wing Wing Phonics is a three-book phonics series designed for elementary school students. The main purpose of this phonics series is to develop basic English sounds through a systematic presentation of the alphabet, vowel combinations, and consonant blends. The series has charming, full-color illustrations and a variety of activities that will stimulate the learners' interest.

Features

· Activities to build listening skills
· Review units featuring fun games
· Chants and stories to review sounds, letters, and words
· A test included in the Teacher's Materials
· A colorful illustrated glossary of key vocabularies
· An accompanying individual workbook with writing activities

Components of the Series

· Wing Wing Phonics 1 Alphabet
· Wing Wing Phonics 2 Single Letter Sounds
· Wing Wing Phonics 3 Long Vowels & Double Letter Sounds

2

Put wings on your phonics!

Wing Wing

Phonics

Answers

Single Letter Sounds

NEXUS Edu

Put wings on your phonics!

Wing Wing

Phonics

2

Single Letter Sounds

Answers

NEXUS Edu

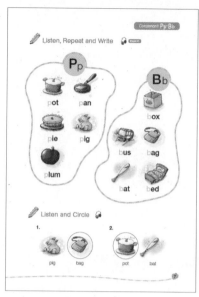

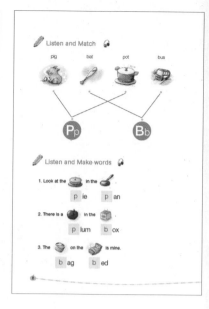

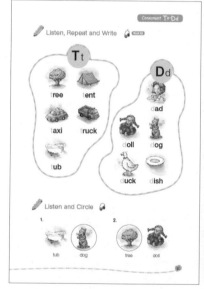

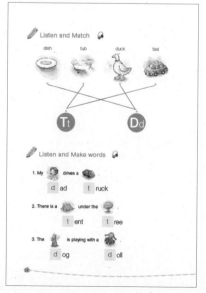

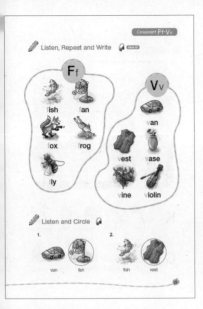

Listen, Repeat and Write

Ff fish fan fox frog fly

Vv van vest vase vine violin

Listen and Circle

1. van fan
2. fish vest

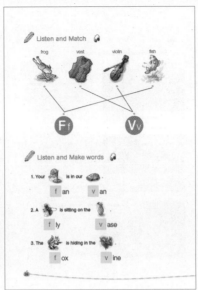

Listen and Match

frog vest violin fish

Ff Vv

Listen and Make words

1. Your ___ is in our ___
   f an   v an

2. A ___ is sitting on the ___
   f ly   v ase

3. The ___ is hiding in the ___
   f ox   v ine

Listen and Read along

Tom and Jane are playing a guessing game.

What is in the vase?

A fish is swimming in the vase.

What is in the vine?

A fox is hiding in the vine.

Wow, you are a genius.

I am smart!

What? What?
What is in the vase?
A fish! A fish!
A fish is swimming in the vase.
What? What?
What is in the vine?
A fox! A fox!
A fox is hiding in the vine.

Make a chant

What? What? What is in the _____?
A_____, A_____.
A_____ is _____ in the _____.

Find the words that begin with "f" and "v" sound in the chant and circle them.

Review

1 Listen and circle the first letter.

bag   plum   truck
Pp (Bb)   Pp Bb   Dd (Tt)

dog   fan   vest
(Dd) Tt   Ff (Vv)   Ff (Vv)

2 Listen and write the letter.

___ish   b ox   f ox

3 Circle the beginning sound.

p b t   d b t   p (b) t

(d) b t   p (f) v   p f (v)

4 Circle the correct picture.

Pp
Tt
Vv

5 Listen and fill in the blanks.

1. Where? Where? Where is the p___le?
   In the p___an. In the p___an.
   The p___le is in the p___an.
   Where? Where? Where is the b___ag?
   On the b___ed. On the b___ed.
   The b___ag is on the b___ed.

2. What? What? What do you have?
   A d___og. A d___og. I have a d___og.
   What? What? What do you have?
   A t___ent. A t___ent. I have a t___ent.

3. What? What? What is in the v___ase?
   A f___ish. A f___ish. A f___ish is swimming in the v___ase.
   What? What? What is in the v___ine?
   A f___ox. A f___ox. A f___ox is hiding in the v___ine.

Let's Play A Game

Play a game with your partner. Use a dice and picture cards(A set).

b, bat

How to Play:
1. Turn all the picture cards upside down and pile them up.
2. Take turns throwing a dice.
3. Draw a card from the deck and read the card.
4. If you can read the card, you score the number that your dice indicates.
   If you can't read, you do not score any.
5. The winner is the one who gets the highest score.

Unit 4 Consonant Hh·Jj

Judy and Mike visit a farm.

Hh ham hen hug hat house

Jj jam jet jug jump jacket

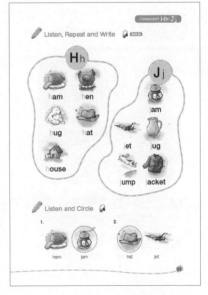

Listen, Repeat and Write

Hh ham hen hug hat house

Jj jam jet jug jump jacket

Listen and Circle

1. ham jam
2. hat jet

3

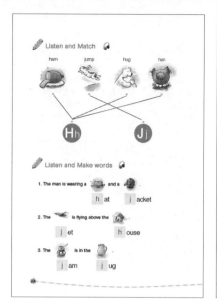

✏️ Listen and Match 🎧

ham   jump   hug   hen

Hh   Jj

✏️ Listen and Make words 🎧

1. The man is wearing a ___ and a ___
   h at   j acket

2. The ___ is flying above the ___
   j et   h ouse

3. The ___ is in the ___
   j am   j ug

🥁 Listen and Read along 🎧

Tom and Jane are playing in the house.

Don't jump in the house.
Sorry. I won't jump in the house.
Don't hug the hen.
Sorry. I won't hug the hen.
It's boring.

Don't. Don't.
Don't jump in the house.
Sorry. I'm sorry.
I won't jump in the house.
Don't. Don't.
Don't hug the hen.
Sorry. I'm sorry.
I won't hug the hen.

🎵 Make a chant
Don't. Don't. Don't ___
Sorry. I'm sorry. I won't ___

🔍 Find the words that begin with "h" and "j" sound in the chant and circle them.

Unit 5 Consonant Kk · Gg

Judy and Mike are having a party.

Kk key kite kiwi king kangaroo

Gg girl glass grape goat gorilla

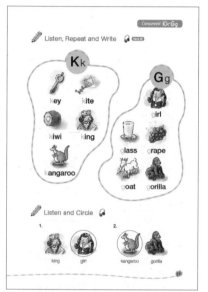

Consonant Kk·Gg

✏️ Listen, Repeat and Write 🎧

Kk
key kite
kiwi king
kangaroo

Gg
girl
glass grape
goat gorilla

✏️ Listen and Circle 🎧

1. king girl   2. kangaroo gorilla

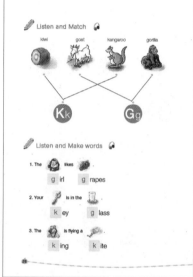

✏️ Listen and Match 🎧

kiwi   goat   kangaroo   gorilla

Kk   Gg

✏️ Listen and Make words 🎧

1. The ___ likes ___
   g irl   g rapes

2. Your ___ is in the ___
   k ey   g lass

3. The ___ is flying a ___
   k ing   k ite

🥁 Listen and Read along 🎧

Tom and Jane are watching the play.

Who has the key?
The king has the key.
The girl has the glass.
Who has the glass?
It was interesting.

Who? Who?
Who has the key?
The king. The king.
The king has the key.
Who? Who?
Who has the glass?
The girl. The girl.
The girl has the glass.

🎵 Make a chant
Who? Who? Who has the ___?
The ___. The ___.
The ___ has the ___.

🔍 Find the words that begin with "k" and "g" sound in the chant and circle them.

Unit 6 Consonant Mm · Nn

Mike is cleaning the house with his sister, Mary.

Mm map man mat mop mud

Nn net nun nuts nest nail

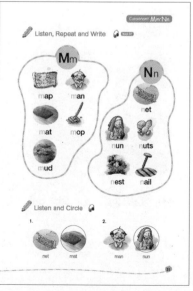

Consonant Mm·Nn

✏️ Listen, Repeat and Write 🎧

Mm
map man
mat mop
mud

Nn
net
nun nuts
nest nail

✏️ Listen and Circle 🎧

1. net mat   2. man nun

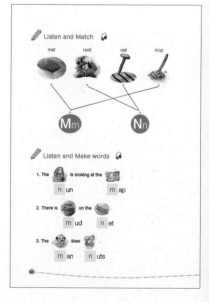

✏️ Listen and Match 🎧

mat   nest   nail   mop

Mm   Nn

✏️ Listen and Make words 🎧

1. The ___ is looking at the ___
   n un   m ap

2. There is ___ on the ___
   m ud   n et

3. The ___ likes ___
   m an   n uts

Listen and Read along

Tom and Jane went to the store to buy something.

Do you need a map?

Yes, I need a map.

Do you need a nail?

No, I don't need a nail.

Do you need?
Do you need a map?
Yes. Yes. I need a map.
Do you need?
Do you need a map?
No. No. I don't need a nail.

♪ **Make a chant**
Do you need? Do you need a _____?
Yes, I need a _____.
(No. No, I don't need a _____.)

♪ Find the words that begin with "m" and "n" sound in the chant and circle them.

1 Listen and circle the first letter.

ham

jet

king

(H h) J j

H h (J j)

G g (K k)

gorilla

net

man

(G g) K k

M m (N n)

(M m) N n

2 Listen and write the letter.

j ump

h ug

m op

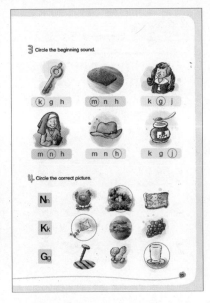

3 Circle the beginning sound.

(k) g h

m (n) h

k (g) j

m (n) h

m n (h)

k g (j)

4 Circle the correct picture.

N n

K k

G g

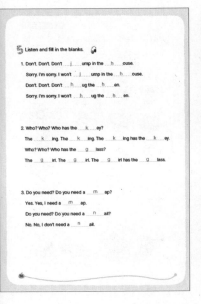

5 Listen and fill in the blanks.

1. Don't. Don't. Don't j ump in the h ouse.
   Sorry. I'm sorry. I won't j ump in the h ouse.
   Don't. Don't. Don't h ug the h en.
   Sorry. I'm sorry. I won't h ug the h en.

2. Who? Who? Who has the k ey?
   The k ing. The k ing. The k ing has the k ey.
   Who? Who? Who has the g lass?
   The g irl. The g irl. The g irl has the g lass.

3. Do you need? Do you need a m ap?
   Yes. Yes, I need a m ap.
   Do you need? Do you need a n ail?
   No. No, I don't need a n ail.

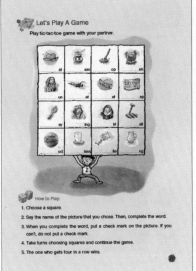

🎲 **Let's Play A Game**
Play tic-tac-toe game with your partner.

at | am | op | en
un | at | at | ap
ey | ing | it | ail
ad | lass | lle | ug

🎲 **How to Play:**
1. Choose a square.
2. Say the name of the picture that you chose. Then, complete the word.
3. When you complete the word, put a check mark on the picture. If you can't, do not put a check mark.
4. Take turns choosing squares and continue the game.
5. The one who gets four in a row wins.

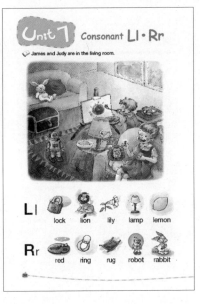

Unit 7 Consonant Ll · Rr

James and Judy are in the living room.

L l lock lion lily lamp lemon

R r red ring rug robot rabbit

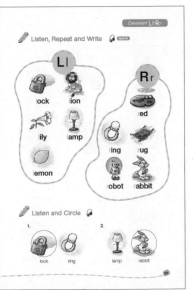

✏ Listen, Repeat and Write

L l

lock ion

R r

red

ily lamp

ring rug

lemon

robot rabbit

✏ Listen and Circle

1. lock ring

2. lamp rabbit

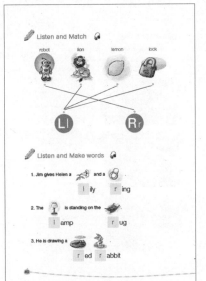

✏ Listen and Match

robot lion lemon lock

L l R r

✏ Listen and Make words

1. Jim gives Helen a _____ and a _____.
   l ily   r ring

2. The _____ is standing on the _____.
   l amp   r ug

3. He is drawing a _____.
   r ed   r abbit

Listen and Read along

Tom and Jane are helping each other.

Is the ring on the rug?

Yes. Yes. The ring is on the rug.

Is the lock on the lamp?

No. The lock isn't on the lamp.

Thank you.

The ring? The ring?
Is the ring on the rug?
Yes. Yes.
The ring is on the rug.
The lock? The lock?
Is the lock on the lamp?
No. No.
The lock isn't on the lamp.

♪ **Make a chant**
The _____. The _____.
Is the _____ on the _____?
Yes. Yes. The _____ is on the _____.
(No. No. The _____ isn't
on the _____.)

♪ Find the words that begin with "l" and "r" sound in the chant and circle them.

Unit 8 — Consonant Ss · Zz

Judy went to the beach with her family.

S s

sun · sea · sky · sand · sleep

Z z

zoo · zero · zigzag · zipper · zebra

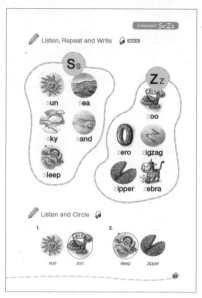

Consonant Ss·Zz

Listen, Repeat and Write

S s

sun · sea
sky · sand
sleep

Z z

zoo
zero · zigzag
zipper · zebra

Listen and Circle

1. sun / zoo
2. sleep / zipper

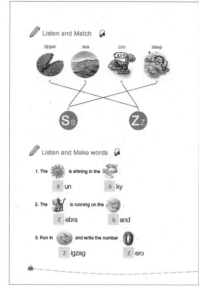

Listen and Match

zipper · sea · zoo · sleep

S s   Z z

Listen and Make words

1. The ___ is shining in the ___.
   s un   s ky

2. The ___ is running on the ___.
   z ebra   s and

3. Run in ___ and write the number ___.
   z igzag   z ero

Listen and Read along

Tom and Jane answer their teacher's question.

I can see the sun in the sky.

Where can you see the sun?

Where can you see the zebra?

I can see the zebra in the zoo.

Good job!

The sun. The sun.
Where can you see the sun?
In the sky. In the sky.
I can see the sun in the sky.
The zebra. The zebra.
Where can you see the zebra?
In the zoo. In the zoo.
I can see the zebra in the zoo.

Make a chant

The ___. The ___.
Where can you see the ___?
In the ___. In the ___.
I can see the ___ in the ___.

Find the words that begin with "s" and "z" sound in the chant and circle them.

Unit 9 — Consonant Cc · Qq

Mike is eating out with his mom.

C c

cup · cat · cap · car · queen

circle · circus · cinema · cereal · quilt

Q q

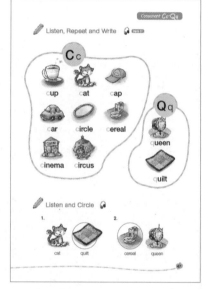

Consonant Cc·Qq

Listen, Repeat and Write

C c

cup · cat · cap
car · circle · cereal
cinema · circus

Q q

queen
quilt

Listen and Circle

1. cat / quilt
2. cereal / queen

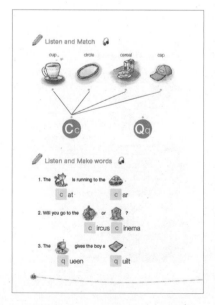

Listen and Match

cup · circle · cereal · cap

C c   Q q

Listen and Make words

1. The ___ is running to the ___.
   c at   c ar

2. Will you go to the ___ or ___?
   c ircus   c inema

3. The ___ gives the boy a ___.
   q ueen   q uilt

Listen and Read along

Mom is angry because Tom and Jane quarreled.

This is my cap.
You can't wear my cap.

This is my quilt.
You can't use my quilt.

This is my cereal.
You can't eat my cereal.

My cap. My cap.
This is my cap.
You can't. You can't.
You can't wear my cap.
My quilt. My quilt.
This is my quilt.
You can't. You can't.
You can't use my quilt.

Make a chant

My ___. My ___.
This is my ___.
You can't. You can't.
You can't wear/use my ___.

Find the words that begin with "c" and "q" sound in the chant and circle them.

Review

1 Listen and circle the first letter.

sun   lock   cup
(Ss) Zz   (Ll) Rr   (Cc) Qq

ring   zoo   queen
Ll (Rr)   Ss (Zz)   (Cc) Qq

2 Listen and write the letter.

___ ky   ___ ily   ___ ircle
s   l   c

3 Circle the beginning sound.

c (s) z   (c) s q   l (r) z

c s (q)   (l) r z   c s (z)

4 Circle the correct picture.

Cc

Rr

Zz

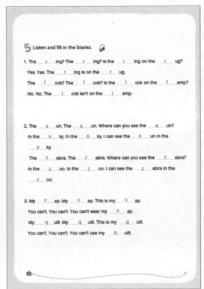

5 Listen and fill in the blanks.

1. The __r__ __ing? The __r__ __ing? Is the __r__ __ing on the __r__ __ug?
   Yes. Yes. The __r__ __ing is on the __r__ __ug.
   The __l__ __ock? The __l__ __ock? Is the __l__ __ock on the __l__ __amp?
   No. No. The __l__ __ock isn't on the __l__ __amp.

2. The __s__ __un. The __s__ __un. Where can you see the __s__ __un?
   In the __s__ __ky. In the __s__ __ky. I can see the __s__ __un in the __s__ __ky.
   The __z__ __ebra. The __z__ __ebra. Where can you see the __z__ __ebra?
   In the __z__ __oo. In the __z__ __oo. I can see the __z__ __ebra in the __z__ __oo.

3. My __c__ __ap. My __c__ __ap. This is my __c__ __ap.
   You can't. You can't. You can't wear my __c__ __ap.
   My __q__ __uilt. My __q__ __uilt. This is my __q__ __uilt.
   You can't. You can't. You can't use my __q__ __uilt.

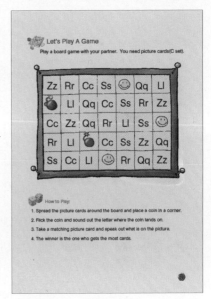

Let's Play A Game

Play a board game with your partner. You need picture cards(C set).

Zz	Rr	Cc	Ss	☺	Qq	Ll
💣	Ll	Qq	Cc	Ss	Rr	Zz
Cc	Zz	Qq	Rr	Ll	Ss	☺
Rr	Ll	💣	Cc	Ss	Zz	Qq
Ss	Cc	Ll	☺	Rr	Qq	Zz

How to Play:
1. Spread the picture cards around the board and place a coin in a corner.
2. Flick the coin and sound out the letter where the coin lands on.
3. Take a matching picture card and speak out what is on the picture.
4. The winner is the one who gets the most cards.

Unit 10 Consonant Ww·Yy·Xx

Mike and Judy are having a good time in the park.

Ww   Yy   Xx

wig web yo-yo yellow fox

wind watch yacht box six

Consonant Ww·Yy·Xx

Listen, Repeat and Write

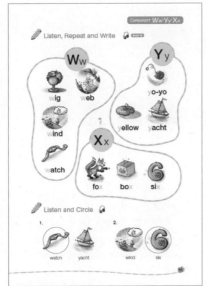

Ww
wig web wind watch

Yy
yo-yo yellow yacht

Xx
fox box six

Listen and Circle

1.   2.

watch yacht   wind six

Listen and Match

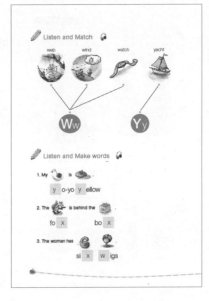

web wind watch yacht

Ww   Yy

Listen and Make words

1. My ___ is ___.
   y o-yo y ellow

2. The ___ is behind the ___.
   fo x bo x

3. The woman has ___.
   si x w igs

Listen and Read along

Tom and Jane made a mess in their house.

Whose watch is this?

The watch is Jane's.

Whose yo-yo is this?

The yo-yo is Tom's.

Whose box is this?

The box is ours.

A watch. A watch.
Whose watch is this?
Jane's. Jane's.
The watch is Jane's.
A yo-yo. A yo-yo.
Whose yo-yo is this?
Tom's. Tom's.
The yo-yo is Tom's.

Make a chant

A ___. A ___.
Whose ___ is this?
___'s. ___'s.
The ___ is ___'s.

Find the words that begin with 'w' and 'y' sound in the chant and circle them.

Unit 11 Short Vowel Aa

Judy went on a picnic with her family.

Aa

ant apple ax arrow actor

rat bat can van dam

Short Vowel Aa

Listen, Repeat and Write

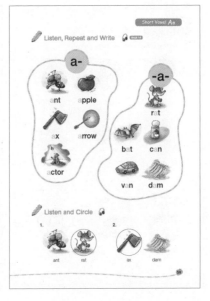

a-
ant apple ax arrow actor

-a-
rat bat can van dam

Listen and Circle

1.   2.

ant rat   ax dam

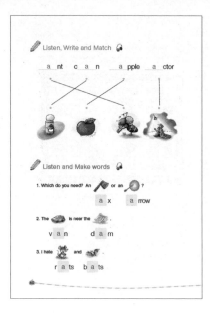

Listen, Write and Match

a nt   c a n   a pple   a ctor

Listen and Make words

1. Which do you need? An [ax] or an [arrow]?
   a x   a rrow

2. The [van] is near the [dam].
   v a n   d a m

3. I hate [rats] and [bats].
   r a ts   b a ts

Listen and Read along

Tom and Jane are afraid of ants and bats.

I don't like ants. I hate ants.
Don't be afraid.
I don't like bats. I hate bats.
Don't be afraid.
I don't like rats. I hate rats.
Don't be afraid.

Ants. Ants.
They are ants.
I don't like ants.
I hate ants.
Bats. Bats.
They are bats.
I don't like bats.
I hate bats.

Make a chant

____(e)s. ____(e)s.
They are ____(e)s.
I don't like ____(e)s.
I hate ____(e)s.

Find the words that have short "a" sound in the chant and circle them.

Unit 12   Short Vowel Ee

Judy and Mike went to the zoo with their friends.

elephant   egg   elevator   elbow   empty

E e

leg   ten   wet   pet   yell

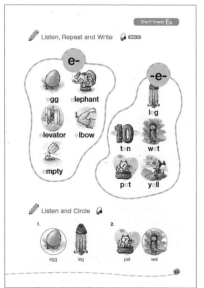

Short Vowel Ee

Listen, Repeat and Write

e-
egg   elephant   elevator   elbow   empty

-e-
leg   ten   wet   pet   yell

Listen and Circle

1. egg   leg
2. pet   wet

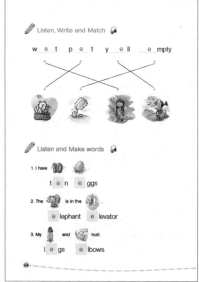

Listen, Write and Match

w et   p et   y ell   e mpty

Listen and Make words

1. I have [ten] [eggs].
   t e n   e ggs

2. The [elephant] is in the [elevator].
   e lephant   e levator

3. My [legs] and [elbows] hurt.
   l e gs   e lbows

Listen and Read along

Tom and Jane got hurt.

My elbows hurt.
Go see a doctor.
My legs hurt.
Go see a doctor.

Elbows. My elbows.
My elbows hurt.
Go. Go.
Go see a doctor.
Legs. My legs.
My legs hurt.
Go. Go.
Go see a doctor.

Make a chant

____(e)s. My ____(e)s.
My ____(e)s hurt.
Go. Go. Go see a doctor.

Find the words that have short "e" sound in the chant and circle them.

Review

1 Listen and write the letter.

w ig   si x   y acht

l e g   a x   d am

2 Listen and circle the first letter.

web   yellow   elephant

Ww Xx   Ww Yy   Aa Ee

3 Circle the correct word.

box / boy / boz   ven / van / vin   ten / tan / tin

nit / ret / rat   wat / wet / wot   pet / pit / pot

4 Circle the correct picture.

Ww
Aa
Ee

5 Listen and fill in the blanks.

1. A [w]atch. A [w]atch. Whose [w]atch is this?
   Jane's. Jane's. The [w]atch is Jane's.
   A [y]o-yo. A [y]o-yo. Whose [y]o-yo is this?
   Tom's. Tom's. The [y]o-yo is Tom's.

2. A[nts]. A[nts]. They are a[nts].
   I don't like a[nts]. I hate a[nts].
   B[ats]. B[ats]. They are b[ats].
   I don't like b[ats]. I hate b[ats].

3. E[lbows]. My e[lbows]. My e[lbows] hurt.
   Go. Go. Go see a doctor.
   L[egs]. My l[egs]. My l[egs] hurt.
   Go. Go. Go see a doctor.

Let's Play A Game

Play a game with your partner.

I.e.g. leg

leg

How to Play:

1. Make word cards using the words that you learned in Unit 10, Unit 11, Unit 12.
2. Spread the word cards that you made on the desk.
3. A teacher chooses a flash card randomly. Then the teacher reads the card out loud.
4. Listen to the word your teacher says. Then try to be the first student to touch the correct word card. The first student takes the word card.
5. The student who gets the most cards wins.

Unit 13 Short Vowel Ii

There was a bazaar in the village.

Ii ink iguana igloo indian insect

sit hit dig mix sing

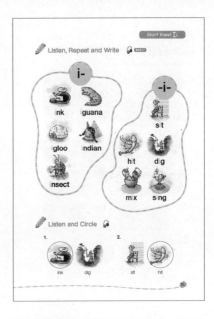

Listen, Repeat and Write

i-
ink iguana
igloo indian
insect

-i-
sit
hit dig
mix sing

Listen and Circle

1. ink dig
2. sit hit

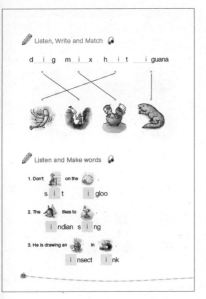

Listen, Write and Match

d i g   m i x   h i t   i guana

Listen and Make words

1. Don't ___ on the ___ .
   s i t   i gloo

2. The ___ likes to ___ .
   i ndian   s i ng

3. He is drawing an ___ in ___ .
   i nsect   i nk

Listen and Read along

Tom and Jane are enjoying their hobbies.

I can hit a ball. It's fun to hit a ball.

I can sing a song. It's fun to sing a song.

Troublemakers!

Hit. Hit.
I can hit a ball.
Fun. Fun.
It's fun to hit a ball.
Sing. Sing.
I can sing a song.
Fun. Fun.
It's fun to sing a song.

Make a chant

I can ___
Fun. Fun. It's fun to ___

Find the words that have short "i" sound in the chant and circle them.

Unit 14 Short Vowel Oo

Judy visits her grandfather.

Oo ox owl octopus ostrich october

mom hot rock sock clock

Listen, Repeat and Write

o-
ox owl
octopus ostrich
october

-o-
mom
hot rock
sock clock

Listen and Circle

1. ox owl
2. rock sock

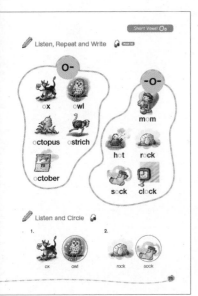

Listen, Write and Match

s o ck cl o ck o ctober o ctopus

Listen and Make words

1. ___ is drinking a cup of ___ coffee.
   M o m   h o t

2. The ___ is kicking a ___ .
   o x   r o ck

3. ___ can fly, but ___ can not fly.
   O wls   o striches

Listen and Read along

Tom and Jane are looking at the birds in the zoo.

An owl is a bird. It can fly.

An ostrich is a bird. It can not fly.

I am faster than a bird.

Owl. Owl.
It is an owl.
An owl is a bird.
It can fly.
Ostrich. Ostrich.
It is an ostrich.
An ostrich is a bird.
It can not fly.

Make a chant

___ ___
It is a/an ___
A/An ___ is a bird.
It can fly. (It can not fly)

Find the words that have short "o" sound in the chant and circle them.

9

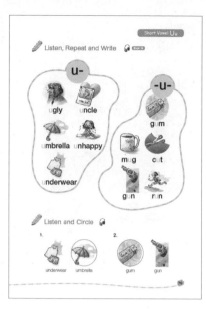

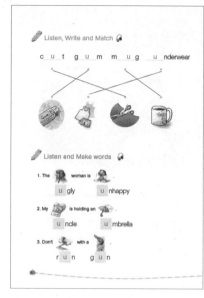

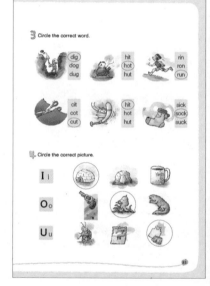

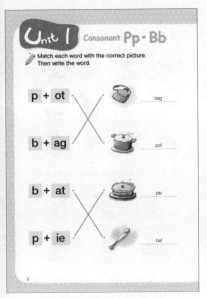

Unit 1 Consonant Pp · Bb

Match each word with the correct picture.
Then write the word.

p + ot
b + ag — bag
b + at — pot
p + ie — pie
— bat

Write the first letter of the word.

p   b   b

p   b   p

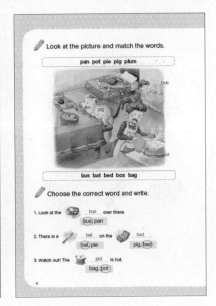

Look at the picture and match the words.

pan pot pie pig plum

bus bat bed box bag

Choose the correct word and write.

1. Look at the ___ bus ___ over there.
   (bus) pan

2. There is a ___ bat ___ on the ___ bed ___.
   (bat, pie)   (pig, bed)

3. Watch out! The ___ pot ___ is hot.
   (bag, pot)

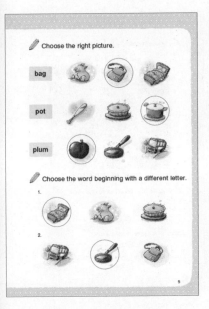

Choose the right picture.

bag

pot

plum

Choose the word beginning with a different letter.

1.

2.

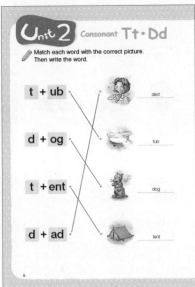

Unit 2 Consonant Tt · Dd

Match each word with the correct picture.
Then write the word.

t + ub — dad
d + og — tub
t + ent — dog
d + ad — tent

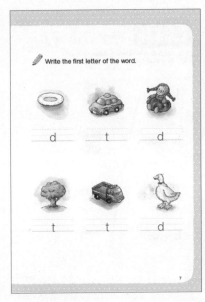

Write the first letter of the word.

d   t   d

t   t   d

Look at the picture and match the words.

tree tent tub taxi truck

dad doll dish dog duck

Choose the correct word and write.

1. Where can I take a ___ taxi ___?
   (taxi) truck

2. The ___ dish ___ is on the table.
   duck, dish

3. My ___ dog ___ is sleeping under the ___ tree ___.
   (dog) tub   (doll, tree)

Choose the right picture.

duck

truck

dish

Choose the word beginning with a different letter.

1.

2.

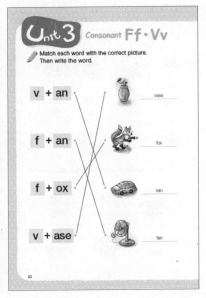

Unit 3 Consonant Ff · Vv

Match each word with the correct picture.
Then write the word.

v + an — vase
f + an — fox
f + ox — van
v + ase — fan

Write the first letter of the word.

f   v   f

v   f   v

Look at the picture and match the words.

fan fox fly frog fish

van vest vine vase violin

Choose the correct word and write.

1. Where can I find a ___ fan ?
fan, van

2. There is a ___ fox in the ___ vine
fox, frog   violin, vine

3. He is wearing a ___ vest
vest, fish

11

12

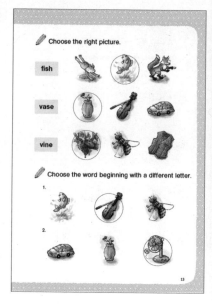

Choose the right picture.

fish

vase

vine

Choose the word beginning with a different letter.

1.

2.

13

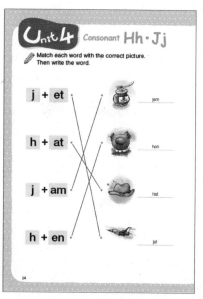

Unit 4 Consonant Hh · Jj

Match each word with the correct picture.
Then write the word.

j + et · · jam

h + at · · hen

j + am · · hat

h + en · · jet

14

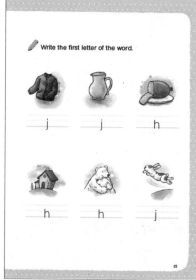

Write the first letter of the word.

j   j   h

h   h   j

15

Look at the picture and match the words.

ham hen hug hat house

jam jet jug jump jacket

Choose the correct word and write.

1. I want to eat a ___ ham sandwich.
ham, jam

2. Don't ___ jump in the classroom.
hug, jump

3. I don't like the ___ hat . I will take the ___ jacket.
hat, jet   house, jacket

16

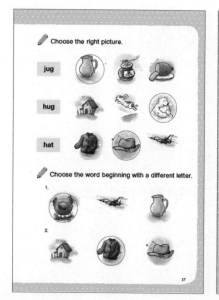

Choose the right picture.

jug

hug

hat

Choose the word beginning with a different letter.

1.

2.

17

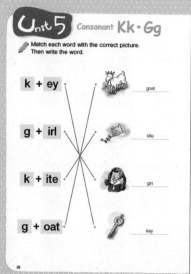

Unit 5 Consonant Kk · Gg

Match each word with the correct picture.
Then write the word.

k + ey · · goat

g + irl · · kite

k + ite · · girl

g + oat · · key

18

Write the first letter of the word.

k   g   k

g   k   g

19

🖊 Look at the picture and match the words.

| key kite kiwi king kangaroo |

🖊 Choose the correct word and write.

1. There is a __kiwi__ on the dish.
   kite, (kiwi)

2. I can't find my __key__ .
   (key), girl

3. The __gorilla__ wants to eat __grape__ s.
   (gorilla), kangaroo   glass, (grape)

20

🖊 Choose the right picture.

kite

girl

goat

🖊 Choose the word beginning with a different letter.

1.

2.

21

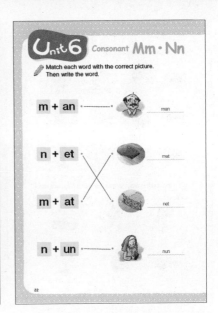

Unit 6 Consonant Mm · Nn

🖊 Match each word with the correct picture.
Then write the word.

m + an ········ man

n + et ········ mat

m + at ········ net

n + un ········ nun

22

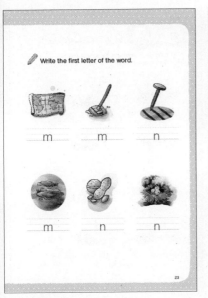

🖊 Write the first letter of the word.

m   m   n

m   n   n

23

🖊 Look at the picture and match the words.

| map man mat mop mud |

| net nun nuts nest nail |

🖊 Choose the correct word and write.

1. Look at the __nest__ .
   (nest), mud

2. It's dirty. Do you have a __mop__ ?
   net, (mop)

3. The __man__ is eating __nuts__ .
   nun, (man)   map, (nuts)

24

🖊 Choose the right picture.

map

net

mud

🖊 Choose the word beginning with a different letter.

1.

2.

25

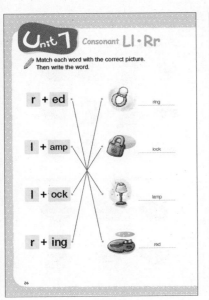

Unit 7 Consonant Ll · Rr

🖊 Match each word with the correct picture.
Then write the word.

r + ed ········ ring

l + amp ········ lock

l + ock ········ lamp

r + ing ········ red

26

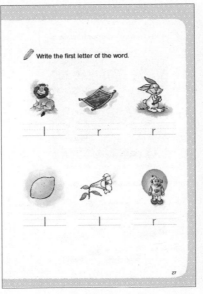

🖊 Write the first letter of the word.

l   r   r

l   l   r

27

🖊 Look at the picture and match the words.

| lock lion lily lamp lemon |

| red ring rug robot rabbit |

🖊 Choose the correct word and write.

1. The __rabbit__ is sleeping on the __rug__ .
   (rabbit), lion   (rug), lamp

2. The __red__ __lily__ is so beautiful!
   (red), lock   ring, (lily)

3. I need to buy a __robot__ and a __lemon__ .
   lamp, (robot)   rabbit, (lemon)

28

13

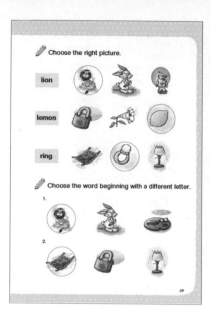

Choose the right picture.

lion

lemon

ring

Choose the word beginning with a different letter.

1.

2.

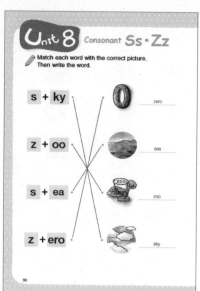

Unit 8 Consonant Ss · Zz

Match each word with the correct picture.
Then write the word.

s + ky   zero

z + oo   sea

s + ea   zoo

z + ero   sky

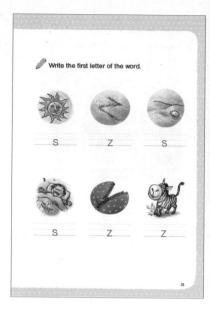

Write the first letter of the word.

s   z   s

s   z   z

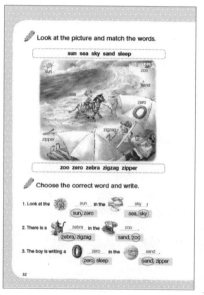

Look at the picture and match the words.

sun sea sky sand sleep

zoo zero zebra zigzag zipper

Choose the correct word and write.

1. Look at the ___ sun ___ in the ___ sky ___
   (sun) zero   sea,(sky)

2. There is a ___ zebra ___ in the ___ zoo ___
   (zebra) zigzag   sand, (zoo)

3. The boy is writing a ___ zero ___ in the ___ sand ___
   (zero) sleep   (sand) zipper

Choose the right picture.

sea

sand

zipper

Choose the word beginning with a different letter.

1.

2.

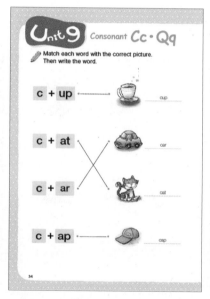

Unit 9 Consonant Cc · Qq

Match each word with the correct picture.
Then write the word.

c + up   cup

c + at   car

c + ar   cat

c + ap   cap

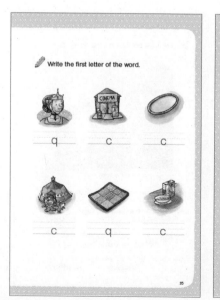

Write the first letter of the word.

q   c   c

c   q   c

Look at the picture and match the words.

cup cat cap car circle

circus cinema cereal queen quilt

Choose the correct word and write them.

1. The ___ cat ___ is wearing a ___ cap ___
   car, (cat)   (cap) cup

2. The ___ queen ___ is making a ___ quilt ___
   (queen) circle   (cereal) (quilt)

3. I will go to the ___ cinema ___ by ___ car ___
   circus, (cinema)   cup,(car)

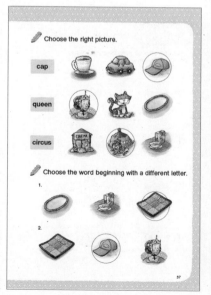

Choose the right picture.

cap

queen

circus

Choose the word beginning with a different letter.

1.

2.

29

30

31

32

33

34

35

36

37

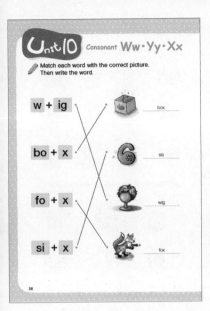

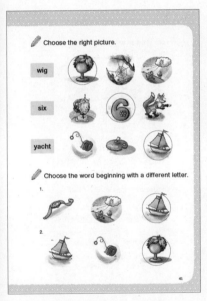

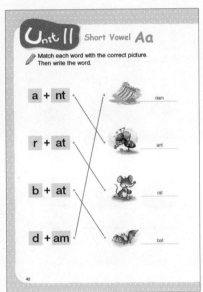

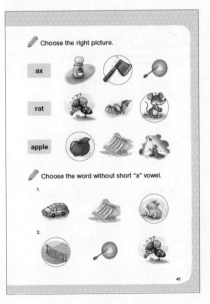

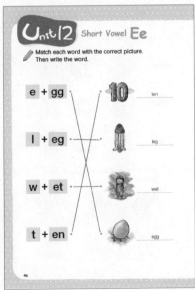

Choose the correct word.

umpty ı **empty**   elephant ı olephant   alevator ı **elevator**

pot ı pot   yİll ı **yell**   **elbow** ı ulbow

47

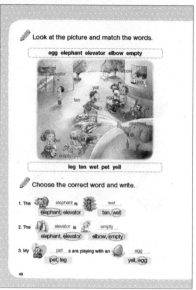

Look at the picture and match the words.

egg elephant elevator elbow empty

leg ten wet pet yell

Choose the correct word and write.

1. The elephant is _wet_
   elephant, elevator   ten, wet

2. The elevator is _empty_
   elephant, elevator   elbow, empty

3. My pet__s are playing with an _egg_
   pet, leg   yell, egg

48

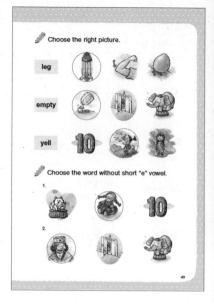

Choose the right picture.

leg

empty

yell

Choose the word without short "e" vowel.

1.

2.

49

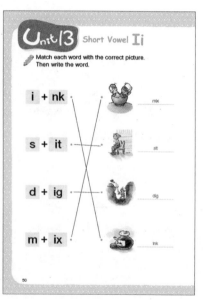

Match each word with the correct picture.
Then write the word.

i + nk   mix

s + it   sit

d + ig   dig

m + ix   ink

50

Choose the correct word.

agloo ı **Igloo**   **Indian** ı undian   seng ı **sing**

oguana ı **iguana**   **insect** ı ensect   hut ı **hit**

51

Look at the picture and match the words.

ink iguana igloo indian insect

sit hit dig mix sing

Choose the correct word and write.

1. Don't _sing_ near my _igloo_
   mix, sing   igloo, indian

2. An iguana _sit_ ting in the tree.
   igloo, iguana   hit, sit

3. An insect is _dig_ ging a hole.
   insect, indian   mix, dig

52

Choose the right picture.

indian

insect

sit

Choose the word without short "i" vowel.

1.

2.

53

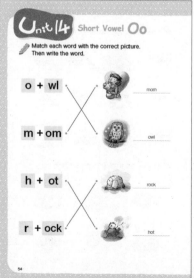

Match each word with the correct picture.
Then write the word.

o + wl   mom

m + om   owl

h + ot   rock

r + ock   hot

54

Choose the correct word.

ox ı ax   uctopus ı **octopus**   sack ı **sock**

ostrich ı istrich   uctober ı **october**   **clock** ı cluck

55

16

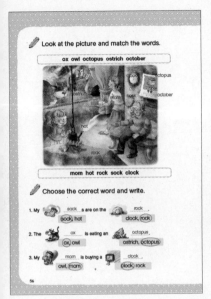

Look at the picture and match the words.

ox owl octopus ostrich october

mom hot rock sock clock

Choose the correct word and write.

1. My __sock__ s are on the __rock__
   (sock), hot   (clock), rock

2. The __ox__ is eating an __octopus__
   (ox), owl   ostrich, (octopus)

3. My __mom__ is buying a __clock__
   owl, (mom)   (clock), rock

56

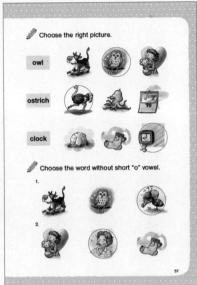

Choose the right picture.

owl

ostrich

clock

Choose the word without short "o" vowel.

1.

2.

57

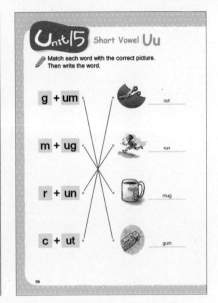

Unit 5 Short Vowel Uu

Match each word with the correct picture.
Then write the word.

g + um   cut

m + ug   run

r + un   mug

c + ut   gum

58

Choose the correct word.

oncle ı (uncle)   umbrella ı ambrella   enderwear ı (underwear)

(gun) ı gin   inhappy ı (unhappy)   egly ı (ugly)

59

Look at the picture and match the words.

ugly uncle umbrella underwear unhappy

gum mug cut gun run

Choose the correct word and write.

1. My __uncle__ is chewing __gum__
   (uncle), ugly   (gum), gun

2. The __ugly__ woman buys an __umbrella__
   uncle, (ugly)   underwear, (umbrella)

3. The __unhappy__ girl __cut__ her hair.
   ugly, (unhappy)   (cut) run

60

Choose the right picture.

uncle

umbrella

run

Choose the word without short "u" vowel.

1.

2.

61

17

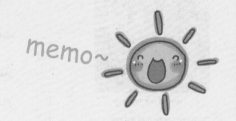

memo~

memo~

Put wings on your phonics! Wing Wing

Phonics 2